KIDS' DAY OUT
Zoos and Animal Parks

Joanne Mattern

RED CHAIR
PRESS

Kids' Day Out is produced and published by Red Chair Press:

Red Chair Press LLC   PO Box 333   South Egremont, MA 01258-0333

www.redchairpress.com

Publisher's Cataloging-In-Publication Data

Names: Mattern, Joanne, 1963–

Title: Zoos and animal parks / Joanne Mattern.

Description: Egremont, MA : Red Chair Press, [2018] | Series: Kids' day out | Interest age level: 007-010. | Includes index and glossary. | Summary: "Where can you go to see lions, and tigers, and bears? You can go to the zoo! A trip to the zoo can be very exciting. A trip to the zoo is also a great way to learn about animal habitats in faraway places."--Provided by publisher.

Identifiers: ISBN 978-1-63440-391-7 (library hardcover) | ISBN 978-1-63440-395-5 (ebook)

Subjects: LCSH: Zoos--History--Juvenile literature. | CYAC: Zoos--History.

Classification: LCC QL76 .M38 2018 (print) | LCC QL76 (ebook) | DDC 590.73--dc23

Illustrations by Tom Sperling

Map illustrations by Joe LeMonnier

Photo credits: Cover, p. 1, 4, 5, 20, 22, 24, 25, 26, 27, 28, 29 :iStock; p. 3, 4, 19, 22, 23, 26, 27, 30, 31: Dreamstime; p. 16, 17, 18: Library of Congress; p. 21: Alamy; p. 30: Ingimage

Printed in the United States of America

0518 1P CGBF18

Contents

Let's Learn About Zoos

Where can you go to see lions, and tigers, and bears? You can go to the zoo! A trip to the zoo can be very exciting. This trip is a chance to see animals you will never find in your backyard or neighborhood park! A trip to the zoo is also a great way to learn about animal habitats in faraway places.

Zoos have been around for thousands of years. In the past, zoos were very different than they are today. Let's take a trip through the amazing history of zoos and animal parks.

Ancient Zoos

Historians think that the first zoo was started by Queen Hatshepsut in 1500 BCE, which was about 3,500 years ago. Queen Hatshepsut ruled Egypt. The queen loved big cats and exotic animals. She sent ships down the coast of Africa. They brought back cheetahs and leopards for the queen's private zoo. The ships also brought back beautiful peacocks and a strange, tall animal called the giraffe.

Emperor Wen Wang ruled China 3,000 years ago. In those days, animals and nature were very important. Wen Wang collected a large number of animals in his private zoo. He called it "The Garden of Intelligence." Wen Wang spent a lot of time in his garden. He thought about nature as he visited alligators, turtles, yaks, pandas, and goats.

A Place to Learn

The ancient Greeks also wanted to understand animals. A wise man called Aristotle collected many animals in his own zoo. He spent hours watching them. He studied what they did and how they behaved. In time, he wrote a book called *The History of Animals* to describe what he learned.

About 2,300 years ago,
a man named Alexander
the Great ruled most of the
known world. Alexander
named the great city of
Alexandria, Egypt, after
himself. The city had many
amazing places, including a huge zoo.
Alexander collected hundreds of animals
for his zoo. These animals included lions,
elephants, ostriches, snakes, and more.

It's a Fact

Ancient Romans kept
small zoos in their homes.
Rich families collected
birds and other animals.
Sometimes they brought
out the animals during
fancy dinner parties!

Gifts Fit for a King

During the 800s, new kings and emperors divided up Europe. Many of these rulers liked having zoos of their own. They often sent unusual animals as gifts to each other.

Around the year 800, an emperor named Charlemagne ruled France and Germany. He asked other rulers to send him animals for his zoo. Charlemagne got gifts from all over the world. One of the most unusual animals was an elephant! Charlemagne had so many animals, it took three zoos to house them all.

Other rulers collected animals in their own zoos too. Kublai Khan, who ruled China during the late 1200s, collected tigers, lynxes, boars, porcupines, deer, and falcons.

Many of England's kings and queens enjoyed zoos. Henry III brought a zoo to the Tower of London in 1230. When the king received three leopards from Frederick II, the Holy Roman Emperor, he put the leopards in the newly named Lion Tower. But only the royal family and their friends were allowed to visit the zoo.

Frederick II, the Holy Roman Emperor, had a large collection of animals. He studied these animals and took them with him when he traveled. In 1254, a number of his animals went with him to Germany for his wedding. These included cheetahs and elephants. All of the animals were decorated with jewels as part of Frederick's wedding parade.

Rulers outside of Europe also enjoyed their zoos. Aztec emperor Moctezuma II built a huge park in Mexico for his animal collection. His zoo included snakes, birds, jaguars, sloths, llamas, and armadillos. More than 600 servants cared for the animals. Moctezuma's zoo was one of the largest in history.

Open to All

Early zoos belonged to kings and emperors. Ordinary people could not go to these personal zoos. That began to change during the 1700s.

The oldest public zoo in the world is the Tiergarten Schonbrunn in Vienna, Austria. It opened in 1752 for the Holy Roman Emperor Francis I and his family. In 1765, the Tiergarten opened to the public.

The 1800s saw more big cities opening public zoos. London opened a public zoo in 1846. So did Paris, Madrid, Stockholm, Melbourne, and many other cities. The first zoo in America opened in Central Park in New York City in 1860.

It's a Fact

In 1889, the National Zoo opened in Washington, D.C. The National Zoo wanted to collect animals from around the world to protect them from extinction. However, the zoo did not have enough money to buy these animals at first. Instead, it exhibited animals that people gave, including raccoons and opossums.

What About Ocean Animals?

People wanted to keep fish, whales, and other ocean animals too. The earliest aquariums were ponds created by the Sumerians, who lived in the Middle East about 4,500 years ago. Later, people learned how to mix air and water so that fish could live in tanks.

The first public aquarium opened in London in 1853. Soon, other cities in Europe built aquariums. The first aquarium in the United States opened in 1856 in New York City. By 1928, there were about 45 aquariums around the world.

Today, many cities have huge aquariums. Visitors can see whales, dolphins, and other large sea creatures. They can attend shows and learn about sea animals. However, some people think it is cruel to keep sea creatures in tanks. Today, many aquariums are doing away with shows and large animal exhibits.

A New Idea

Animals who lived in these early zoos did not have happy lives. They were kept in cages. Some cages were too small for the animals to stand and walk around. There was nothing to do. The animals were lonely and bored. Many times zookeepers fed them the wrong kind of food. People didn't know much about what the animals should eat.

In 1907, Carol Hagenbeck opened a new kind of zoo near Hamburg, Germany. Hagenbeck did not keep his animals in cages. Instead, they were free to roam outside. Walls, rocks, and deep moats kept the animals away from people. For the first time, people could watch animals living in a more natural way.

Scientists and zookeepers soon changed their ideas of what a zoo should be. Modern zoos built exhibits where animals could live as they did in the wild. Exhibits included hiding places, hills, and rocks. Monkeys had trees to climb. Tigers had caves to sleep in. Birds lived in forests with plenty of trees and room to fly.

Scientists also worked to make the animals happier. They gave them toys to play with and puzzles to solve. Instead of feeding the animals in bowls, they hid food around the exhibit for the animals to find, much like they do in the wild.

Zoos also became places to protect and save animal species. In the past, hunters captured animals from their habitats and brought them to zoos in big cities. During the late 1900s, zoos started breeding their own animals. They also shared animals with other zoos so that more baby animals could be born.

It's a Fact

More giant pandas live in China than anywhere else. Over the years, China has sent some of these pandas to zoos in the United States and Europe. This program helps bring pandas to zoos all over the world so more people can see them.

Golden lion tamarin in Brazil

Some zoos bred animals and then released them into the wild. This was a good way to keep animals from becoming extinct. In 1981, scientists in Brazil bred hundreds of golden lion tamarins. Then they released them into the wild. They hope to have 2,000 tamarins living in the wild by 2025.

Other zoos breed animals that may never be able to live in the wild. The Bali Bird Park shelters rare birds from all over Asia, Africa, and South America. These birds may not have a place to live in the wild, but living in a zoo keeps them from becoming extinct.

Today, many zoos have become wildlife parks. Animals in these parks are free to roam and live like they do in the wild. When people drive through the parks, they can see animals living in real habitats. Zoo exhibits and the people who work there also educate the public about animals and their habitats.

A New Zoo

Things have changed a lot since the first zoos were created more than 4,000 years ago. In the past, only rulers and rich people could afford to have zoos. Later, zoos became places that were open to the public. However, as more people visited zoos, they saw that the animals were unhappy. In the past 100 years, the best zoos have changed into places that put animals first. They can even save the lives of a whole species!

It would be great if all animals could live in the wild. Sadly, the loss of natural habitats and other problems make this impossible. Good zoos give animals a chance to survive. And they give people a chance to see amazing creatures up close. A zoo is a great place to have fun— and learn—on a kids' day out!

Glossary

ancient very old

aquariums buildings with tanks of water where fish and other sea animals are kept

breed to mate and have babies

emperors powerful rulers of empires

exhibited showed in public

exotic strange and unusual

extinction dying out forever

habitats natural homes of animals and plants

private not open to the public

species a group of animals that are the same

Learn More in the Library

Books

Krull, Kathleen. *What's New? The Zoo*. Arthur Levine Books, 2014.

Maxwell, Cassandre. *Fur, Fins, and Feathers*. Eerdmans Books for Young Readers, 2015.

Web Sites

American Library Association: Web sites for kids
http://gws.ala.org/category/animals/zoos-aquariums

Smithsonian National Zoo, Washington, D.C.
https://nationalzoo.si.edu

National Aquarium, Baltimore, MD
https://aqua.org

Index

About the Author

Joanne Mattern is the author of many nonfiction books for children. She enjoys writing about animals, history, and famous people and loves to bring science and history to life for young readers. Joanne lives in New York State with her husband, four children, and several pets and enjoys reading and music.